Good Housekeeping Cookery Club

VEGETARIAN

Linda Yewdall

EBURY PRESS
LONDON

First published 1994

1 3 5 7 9 10 8 6 4 2

First published in the United Kingdom in 1994 by Ebury Press
Random House, 20 Vauxhall Bridge Road, London SW1V 2SA

Random House Australia (Pty) Limited
20 Alfred Street, Milsons Point, Sydney,
New South Wales 2061, Australia

Random House New Zealand Limited
18 Poland Road, Glenfield,
Auckland 10, New Zealand

Random House South Africa (Pty) Limited
PO Box 337, Bergvlei, South Africa

Random House UK Limited Reg. No. 954009

A CIP catalogue record for this book is available from the British Library.

Managing Editor: JANET ILLSLEY
Design: SARA KIDD
Special Photography: JAMES MURPHY
Food Stylist: ALLYSON BIRCH
Photographic Stylist: ROISIN NIELD
Techniques Photography: KARL ADAMSON
Food Techniques Stylist: ANNIE NICHOLS
Recipe Testing: EMMA-LEE GOW

This collection includes a number of
recipes which have been especially created
for vegetarians by the GOOD HOUSEKEEPING INSTITUTE

ISBN 0-09-178428-X

Typeset in Gill Sans by Textype Typesetters, Cambridge
Colour Separations by Magnacraft, London
Printed and bound in Italy by New Interlitho Italia S.p.a., Milan

CONTENTS

COOKERY NOTES

- Both metric and imperial measures are given for the recipes. Follow either metric or imperial throughout as they are not interchangeable.
- All spoon measures are level unless otherwise stated. Sets of measuring spoons are available in metric and imperial for accurate measurement of small quantities.
- Ovens should be preheated to the specified temperature. Grills should also be preheated. The cooking times given in the recipes assume that this has been done.
- Where a stage is specified in brackets under freezing instructions, the dish should be frozen at the end of that stage.
- Size 2 eggs should be used except where otherwise specified.
- Use freshly ground black pepper unless otherwise specified.
- Use fresh rather than dried herbs unless dried herbs are suggested in the recipe.

INTRODUCTION

People embrace vegetarianism for a variety of reasons. For George Bernard Shaw it was Shelley 'who opened my eyes to the savagery of my diet'. In the poet's words 'Never again may blood of bird or beast stain with its venomous stream a human feast'! Several religions advocate vegetarianism, including Hindu, Sikh and seventh day Adventist.

Others, for health reasons, decide that avoiding meat and fish has many attractions. A vegetarian diet by its very nature is low in saturated animal fat and high in fibre. There is also a move away from diets which are very high in protein, and this is where the humble pulses come into their own. Combine pulses in the same course with vegetables, grains, nuts and dairy products, and together they provide all the amino acids you need to compare favourably with the first class protein found in meat and fish.

There are different kings of vegetarian diets. Lacto-vegetarians avoid meat and fish, but they will include milk and dairy products. In addition, lacto-ovo vegetarians eat eggs. The four main food groups within a lacto-vegetarian diet are: beans, nuts and seeds; grains; diary produce; fruit and vegetables. To eat a balanced diet you need to include some foods from each group every day to ensure you are getting all the nutrients your body needs.

Vegans – often referred to as 'strict vegetarians' – won't eat any product which has involved the exploitation of animals. This includes dairy products, eggs, meat, fish, and even products such as honey. Special care must be taken to maintain a well balanced vegan diet, as dietary deficiencies can occur in protein, calcium, iron and vitamin B12.

Care should always be taken in the preparation and cooking of fruit and vegetables because up to 50% of the vitamin content can be lost, especially if they are overcooked. Wash and lightly scrub or thinly peel the vegetables just prior to gentle steaming or simmering in the minimum amount of water. Always retain the cooking water for stock. Avoid the excess use of salt, too.

The secret of successful vegetarian cooking in my opinion is to mix and match a variety of ordinary and exciting ingredients together, with always the marriage of flavours and textures firmly in mind. Luckily the days of nut cutlets and vegetarian food masquerading as meat have long gone. Now the humble vegetable takes its rightful place and the 'meat and two veg' scenario is a thing of the past.

The beauty of vegetarian cookery is that the ground rules adhered to by meat eaters need not apply, as the absence of meat and fish allows for a freer style of eating. Experiment with the wide variety of interesting and unusual ingredients available today. Sea vegetables, for example, are one of the oldest crops and can be relied on to supply ample vitamins, essential amino acids and trace elements, especially iodine. Agar Agar is made from a variety of seaweeds and makes a good substitute for animal gelatine. Seeds, nuts and pulses of every size, type and hue are a valuable storecupboard source of protein-packed pleasure. A huge bowl of salad is always well received, either as a course on its own or as an accompaniment to the main course. Life need never be dull as a vegetarian, as long as you eat a wide variety of foods.

DRIED PULSES

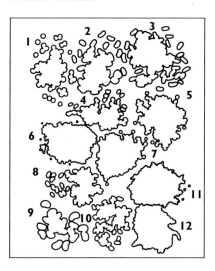

1 Chick Peas; *2* Red Kidney Beans; *3* White Kidney Beans; *4* Black-eyed Beans; *5* Split Peas; *6* Red Lentils; *7* Green Lentils; *8* Cannellini Beans; *9* Butter Beans; *10* Flageolet Beans; *11* Yellow Lentils; *12* Puy Lentils.

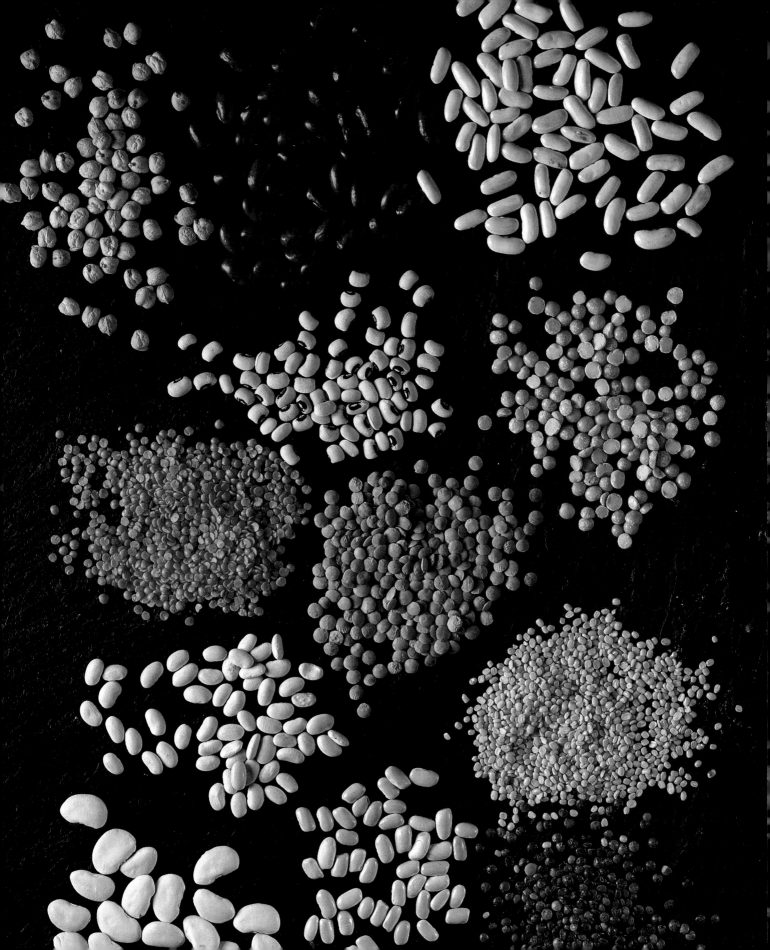

PREPARING VEGETABLES

When choosing vegetables, look for a good bright colour and crispness – as indications of freshness. Avoid vegetables that show signs of discolouration. In general, the younger and smaller the vegetable the sweeter and more tender it will be, although you may find that some of the baby vegetables lack flavour owing to their immaturity. Always clean vegetables thoroughly; those with inedible skins must, of course, be peeled too. Sharp knives and a heavy chopping board are essential for cutting.

SHREDDING VEGETABLES

Leafy vegetables, such as cabbage, spring greens and spinach, are often shredded before cooking.

1. To shred a cabbage, quarter, then cut out the core.

2. Place cut-side down on a board and cut vertically into shreds.

DICING VEGETABLES

Peel if necessary and cut into small uniform squares. To dice an onion, proceed as follows:

1. Peel, leaving the root end intact. Halve vertically then lay one half, cut-side down, on a board.

2. Slice the onion horizontally towards the root, but not right through.

3. Slice vertically, keeping the root end intact.

4. Cut the onion crosswise into dice.

VEGETABLE JULIENNE

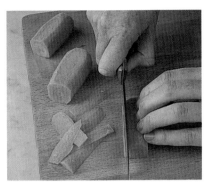

1. Peel if necessary, then trim off all rounded edges. Cut into 6 cm (2½ inch) lengths

2. Using a cook's knife, cut these lengths into 3 mm (⅛ inch) slices.

3. Stack 4 or 5 slices on top of each other and cut into 3 mm (⅛ inch) strips.

DIAGONAL SLICING

Cut the vegetable at an oblique angle into 5 mm (¼ inch) slices.

DECORATIVE SLICING

1. Remove strips of peel lengthwise at regular intervals, using a canelle knife.

2. Cut crosswise into slices.

VEGETABLE RIBBONS

Using a vegetable peeler and pressing firmly, peel whole lengths to make ribbons. This technique works well with carrots and courgettes.

CLEANING LEEKS

Leeks are not easy to clean, because dirt gets trapped between their tightly rolled layers. The following method works well.

1. Trim off the root and top, then slit lengthwise into halves or quarters, leaving the root end intact.

2. Hold several prepared leeks by the root end and place in a bowl of cold water. Shake thoroughly to loosen any dirt.

3. Rinse thoroughly under cold running water.

PREPARING ASPARAGUS

This applies to medium spears; fine asparagus doesn't need peeling.

1. Using a vegetable peeler, shave the length of each stalk from just below the tip to the base.

2. Break off the woody ends. Trim spears to roughly the same length.

3. Divide into bundles of 6-8 spears and tie with string.

DEGORGING AUBERGINES

1. Cut the aubergines into slices and layer in a colander, sprinkling each layer liberally with salt. Leave to degorge the bitter juices.

2. After 30 minutes, rinse thoroughly under cold running water.

3. Pat the aubergine slices dry with kitchen paper.

PEELING TOMATOES

I. Mark a shallow cross on the bottom of each tomato.

2. With a sharp knife, cut out the core.

3. Place in a bowl, pour on boiling water to cover and leave for 10-20 seconds, depending on ripeness.

4. Using a slotted spoon, transfer the tomatoes to a bowl of cold water to cool quickly.

5. Take out each tomato and peel off the skin – it should come away easily.

6. To seed a tomato, halve crosswise and squeeze to remove the seeds.

PEELING PEPPERS

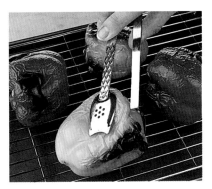

I. Grill whole peppers, turning occasionally until blistered and charred all over.

2. Transfer the peppers to a board and cover with a damp tea towel (the steam helps to lift the skins).

3. When cool enough to handle, peel away the skins using a sharp knife.

Red pepper and sweet potato soup

The Mediterranean roasted red pepper blends perfectly with the Caribbean sweet potato in this flavourful soup. I have roasted the peppers to enhance the flavour and included freshly shredded basil leaves. Serve the soup with plenty of crusty bread as a nourishing and warming starter.

SERVES 4

2 large red peppers, total
  weight about 450 g (1 lb)
225 g (8 oz) sweet potato
squeeze of lemon juice
1 onion
2 garlic cloves
225 g (8 oz) tomatoes, or
  200 g (7 oz) can plum
  tomatoes
15 ml (1 tbsp) extra-virgin
  olive oil
900 ml (1½ pint) vegetable
  stock
coarse sea salt and pepper
TO SERVE
60 ml (4 tbsp) natural
  yogurt
30 ml (2 tbsp) finely
  shredded fresh basil
basil leaves, to garnish

PREPARATION TIME
10-15 minutes
COOKING TIME
30 minutes
FREEZING
Suitable

150 CALS PER SERVING

1. Preheat the grill to hot, or preheat the oven to 190°C (375°F) Mark 5. Grill or roast the peppers on a rack, turning frequently, for 15-20 minutes until the skin is blistered and blackened. Cover with a damp cloth and leave to cool slightly.

2. Meanwhile, peel the sweet potato, cut into small pieces and immediately immerse in a bowl of cold water with a little lemon juice added to prevent discolouration. Add the sweet potato to a pan of boiling water and simmer for 10-15 minutes until tender. Drain.

3. Meanwhile, peel the roasted peppers, reserving some of the strips of blackened skin for the garnish if desired. Holding them over a bowl to catch the juices, halve the peppers, then remove the core and seeds. Cut the peppers into slices. Peel and finely chop the onion and garlic.

4. Immerse fresh tomatoes in a bowl of boiling water for 30 seconds, then remove with a slotted spoon, allow to cool slightly and peel away the skins.

5. Heat the oil in a large saucepan and fry the onion and garlic until softened. Add the peppers and reserved juices, tomatoes, sweet potatoes and two thirds of the stock. Season with salt and pepper to taste and cook for 5-10 minutes.

6. Transfer the soup to a blender or food processor and work until smooth. Return to the cleaned saucepan and reheat, adding more vegetable stock as required to achieve the desired consistency. Adjust the seasoning and add a squeeze of lemon juice, to taste.

7. To serve, divide the soup between warmed serving bowls and add a swirl of yogurt to each portion. Sprinkle with the shredded basil, and tiny pieces of blackened pepper skin if desired. Add a generous grind of pepper and garnish with basil leaves. Serve with crusty bread.

NOTE: You can use ordinary potato in place of the sweet potato, if you prefer, though the soup will lose its sweetness.

TECHNIQUE

After grilling or roasting the peppers, cover them with a damp cloth; the steam helps to lift the skin.

CHILLED AVOCADO AND LIME SOUP

Avocado, with its wonderful buttery texture, is a favourite fruit. Rich in vitamin A and potassium, it is however unfortunately high in fat which accounts for a hefty calorie count – 240 calories per 100 g! Here I've combined avocado with fresh lime juice to cut through the richness, and added a swirl of fromage frais and a sprinkling of chives to serve. Melba toast, made from a robust stoneground wholemeal loaf, would be an ideal accompaniment.

SERVES 4

1 bunch of spring onions
15 ml (1 tbsp) extra-virgin
    olive oil
225 g (8 oz) potato
900 ml (1½ pints) vegetable
    stock
1-2 limes
2 ripe avocados
30 ml (2 tbsp) fromage frais
    (preferably 0% fat)
coarse sea salt and pepper
TO SERVE
60 ml (4 tbsp) fromage frais
    (preferably 0% fat)
snipped chives, to garnish

PREPARATION TIME
5-10 minutes, plus chilling
COOKING TIME
20 minutes
FREEZING
Not suitable

235 CALS PER SERVING

1. Trim the spring onions, then finely slice both the green and white parts. Heat the oil in a large saucepan, add the spring onions and fry gently until softened.

2. Meanwhile, peel the potato and cut into small pieces. Add to the softened onions and fry, stirring, for 2 minutes. Add the stock and bring to the boil. Cover and simmer for 15-20 minutes.

3. Towards the end of the cooking time, remove a little zest from one of the limes, using a zester, and set aside for the garnish. Squeeze the juice from the lime. Halve, stone and peel the avocados, then chop roughly. Add the avocado to the soup with the lime juice. Taste and adjust the seasoning; add extra lime juice (from the other lime) if required.

4. Take the soup off the heat, allow to cool slightly, then transfer to a blender or food processor. Work until smooth, then add the fromage frais and stir to mix. Pour into individual soup bowls and chill in the refrigerator for 3-4 hours. (The soup thickens as it is chilled.)

5. To serve, add a swirl of fromage frais and a squeeze of lime juice. Grind some black pepper on top and garnish with snipped chives and the lime zest. Serve with Melba toast, or bread rolls.

NOTE: Omit the fromage frais to make this recipe suitable for vegans.

MELBA TOAST: Cut 4-5 thin slices from a day-old loaf of wholemeal bread. Toast lightly on both sides. Quickly cut off the crusts and split each slice in two horizontally. Bake in a preheated oven at 180°C (350°F) Mark 4 for 10-15 minutes until crisp and curled.

VARIATION

Add a trimmed bunch of watercress to the spring onions with the potato. Use the juice of ½ lime only.

TECHNIQUE

For the garnish, finely pare strips of lime rind using a zester.

Mushroom Pâté with Madeira

This is a rich mushroom pâté, flavoured with dried porcini and a variety of fresh mushrooms. You can use any combination of mushrooms, but try to include some flavourful wild ones or cultivated dark field mushrooms. Don't be tempted to use all button mushrooms as the end result will lack colour and flavour. Serve the pâté with hot olive bread, ciabatta, French bread or toast.

SERVES 6

15 g (½ oz) dried porcini
    mushrooms (see note)
150 ml (¼ pint) milk
1 small onion
1 garlic clove (optional)
25 g (1 oz) butter
coarse sea salt and pepper
350 g (12 oz) mushrooms
125 g (4 oz) ricotta cheese
15 ml (1 tbsp) Madeira
2.5 ml (½ tsp) balsamic
    vinegar or lemon juice
5 ml (1 tsp) mushroom
    ketchup
freshly grated nutmeg, to
    taste
15-30 ml (1-2 tbsp) chopped
    fresh parsley or coriander
    (optional)
TO GARNISH
chopped parsley or
    coriander

PREPARATION TIME
15 minutes, plus soaking
COOKING TIME
20-25 minutes
FREEZING
Not suitable

100 CALS PER SERVING

1. Rinse the porcini under cold running water to wash away the grit, then place in a bowl. Pour on the warm milk and leave to soak for 20 minutes. Drain the porcini and chop finely.

2. Peel and finely chop the onion and garlic, if using. Melt the butter in a saucepan, add the onion and garlic and fry gently for 5-10 minutes until softened and transparent. Season with salt and pepper.

3. Meanwhile, wipe the fresh mushrooms with a damp cloth to clean them, then chop finely.

4. Add the porcini and fresh mushrooms to the onion and garlic, increase the heat a little and cook, stirring occasionally, for about 15 minutes until the mushrooms are tender and reduced to a thick pulp. Leave to cool slightly.

5. Transfer the mushroom mixture to a food processor or bowl. Add the ricotta, Madeira, balsamic vinegar, mushroom ketchup and nutmeg and process very briefly or stir until evenly mixed; the pâté should retain a coarse texture. Stir in the chopped parsley or coriander if using. Adjust the seasoning.

6. Turn into a serving dish or individual ramekins and garnish with parsley or coriander. Serve with olive bread, ciabatta, French bread or toast.

NOTE: If dried porcini are unobtainable, use an extra 125 g (4 oz) flavourful fresh mushrooms.

TECHNIQUE

Rinse the porcini under cold running water to wash away the grit.

CARROT AND CORIANDER ROULADE

This savoury carrot cake makes an interesting and sustaining starter. The carrot roulade is rolled around a tasty filling of cream cheese flavoured with garlic, herbs and chopped coriander leaves. Serve it in slices with a mixed leaf and herb salad, and toasted granary or walnut bread.

SERVES 4-6

50 g (2 oz) butter or
    vegetable margarine
450 g (1 lb) carrots, grated
4 eggs (size 2), separated
15 ml (1 tbsp) chopped
    coriander leaves
coarse sea salt and pepper
FILLING
175 g (6 oz) soft cheese
    flavoured with garlic and
    herbs
15 ml (1 tbsp) chopped
    coriander leaves
30-45 ml (2-3 tbsp) crème
    fraîche
TO SERVE
assorted salad leaves
herb sprigs, such as dill and
    chervil or parsley

PREPARATION TIME
30 minutes
COOKING TIME
10-15 minutes
FREEZING
Not suitable

340-230 CALS PER SERVING

1. Preheat the oven to 200°C (400°F) Mark 6. Line a 30 x 20 cm (12 x 8 inch) Swiss roll tin with non-stick baking parchment. Coarsely grate the carrots, using a grating disc in a food processor, or by hand.

2. Melt the butter or margarine in a pan, add the carrots and cook gently, stirring frequently, for 5 minutes or until slightly coloured. Transfer to a bowl, allow to cool slightly, then add the egg yolks and coriander and beat well. Season with salt and pepper.

3. Whisk the egg whites in a bowl until firm peaks form, then stir 30 ml (2 tbsp) into the carrot mixture to lighten it. Carefully fold in the rest of the egg whites.

4. Spread the mixture evenly in the prepared tin and bake in the oven for 10-15 minutes until risen and firm to the touch. Turn out onto a sheet of non-stick baking parchment, cover with a clean, damp cloth and allow to cool.

5. Meanwhile, prepare the filling. Put the soft cheese in a bowl. Using a fork, mix in the chopped coriander and enough crème fraîche to yield a smooth, spreading consistency. Taste and adjust the seasoning if necessary.

6. Remove the cloth from the roulade. Spread evenly with the filling, leaving a 1 cm (½ inch) border all round. Carefully roll up from a short side, using the paper to help.

7. To serve, cut the roulade into slices and arrange on individual plates with the salad leaves and herbs.

VARIATION

Bake the carrot mixture in two 18 cm (7 inch) sandwich tins. Turn out and cool on a wire rack, then sandwich together with the filling.

TECHNIQUE

Lightly fold the whisked egg whites into the roulade mixture, using a large metal spoon.

GRILLED TOMATO AND MOZZARELLA SALAD

This hot salad starter can be prepared ahead, chilled, then grilled just before serving. Make sure you use tomatoes which are ripe and have plenty of flavour – it does make a difference. If you are buying from a supermarket, look for the packs marked 'grown for flavour'.

SERVES 4

175 g (6 oz) aubergine
45 ml (3 tbsp) olive oil
450 g (1 lb) tomatoes
150 g (5 oz) mozzarella
  cheese
60 ml (4 tbsp) torn fresh
  basil leaves
finely grated rind of 1 lemon
5 ml (1 tsp) lemon juice
salt and pepper
TO GARNISH
basil leaves

PREPARATION TIME
10 minutes
COOKING TIME
About 10 minutes
FREEZING
Not suitable

240 CALS PER SERVING

1. Preheat the grill. Cut the aubergine into thin slices. Brush very lightly with some of the olive oil and place on the grill rack. Grill the aubergine slices on both sides until they are crisp and golden brown; do not let them turn too dark at this stage.

2. Thinly slice the tomatoes. Cut the mozzarella cheese into thin slices.

3. In a bowl, whisk together the remaining olive oil, torn basil, lemon rind and juice. Season with salt and pepper.

4. Arrange the tomato, aubergine and mozzarella slices, overlapping in a single layer, in a large shallow flameproof dish. Spoon the dressing evenly over the top.

5. Place under a hot grill for 3-4 minutes or until the mozzarella begins to melt. Sprinkle with salt and pepper and garnish with basil leaves. Serve immediately, accompanied by warm crusty bread.

VARIATION

Instead of basil, flavour the salad with 45 ml (3 tbsp) snipped chives or chopped coriander leaves.

TECHNIQUE

Layer the aubergine, tomato and mozzarella slices in the dish, overlapping them.

WATERCRESS AND WENSLEYDALE TARTLETS

Mild, crumbly Wensleydale cheese is teamed with peppery watercress in these tasty tartlets. The unique flavour of watercress needs a mellow companion and Wensleydale is an ideal one. The tartlets are best served piping hot direct from the oven. Surround them with sprigs of watercress and chervil or parsley.

SERVES 4

PASTRY

125 g (4 oz) plain wholemeal
    flour
125 g (4 oz) plain flour
pinch of salt
pinch of mustard powder
125 g (4 oz) butter or
    vegetable margarine
1 egg (size 3), beaten

FILLING

6 spring onions
75 g (3 oz) watercress
15 ml (1 tbsp) sunflower oil
2 eggs
150 ml (¼ pint) milk
125 g (4 oz) Wensleydale
    cheese, finely grated
30 ml (2 tbsp) chopped fresh
    chervil or parsley
coarse sea salt and pepper
freshly grated nutmeg

TO GARNISH

watercress sprigs
chervil or parsley sprigs

PREPARATION TIME
20 minutes, plus chilling
COOKING TIME
30-35 minutes
FREEZING
Suitable

690 CALS PER SERVING

1. To make the pastry, sift the flours, salt and mustard powder into a bowl. Rub in the butter, using your fingertips, until the mixture resembles fine breadcrumbs. Using a round-bladed knife stir in the egg and sufficient chilled water to mix; you will need about 15-30 ml (1-2 tbsp). When the dough begins to stick together in large lumps, gather it together and form into a ball. Wrap in cling film and chill in the refrigerator for 30 minutes.

2. Roll out the pastry and use to line four individual loose-bottomed 10 cm (4 inch) fluted flan tins. Chill for 20 minutes. Preheat the oven to 200°F (400°C) Mark 6. Line the flan cases with greaseproof paper and baking beans and bake blind for 15 minutes.

3. Meanwhile make the filling. Trim the spring onions and slice finely. Trim the watercress and chop finely. Heat the oil in a saucepan, add the spring onions and fry gently for about 5 minutes until softened. Add the watercress to the pan and cook for 1 minute only.

4. Beat the eggs and milk together in a bowl with the grated cheese. Stir in the watercress and onion mixture, then add the chopped chervil or parsley and salt and pepper to taste.

5. Lower the oven temperature to 190°C (375°F) Mark 5. Spoon the filling into the pastry cases, sprinkle with freshly grated nutmeg and bake in the oven for 15-20 minutes until risen and just set. Serve immediately, garnished with watercress and chervil or parsley.

NOTE: Alternatively the tartlets can be served cold. Remove from their cases after baking and cool on a wire rack.

TECHNIQUE

Line four 10 cm (4 inch) individual flan tins with the wholemeal pastry, gently pressing it into the fluted edges.

MIXED LEAF SALAD WITH HERB DRESSING

Make this huge, colourful salad in a large glass dish or salad bowl. Search out exciting leaves with colour, texture and flavour. The secret of a good salad is to tear – rather than chop – the leaves, and finely shred the rest of the ingredients – with the exception of the cherry tomatoes. The dressing unlike the salad is understated: use the very best olive oil and balsamic vinegar if possible.

SERVES 6

½ cos lettuce

75 g (3 oz) mixed salad leaves, such as lamb's lettuce, oak leaf lettuce and batavia

40 g (1½ oz) rocket leaves

1 carrot

½ head of fennel

2 celery sticks

1 courgette

225 g (8 oz) cherry tomatoes

1 head of chicory

1 small red onion, peeled

DRESSING

175 ml (6 fl oz) extra-virgin olive oil

30 ml (2 tbsp) balsamic vinegar or wine vinegar

5 ml (1 tsp) Dijon mustard

2.5 ml (½ tsp) sugar

coarse sea salt and pepper

30 ml (2 tbsp) chopped chervil, parsley or dill

TO GARNISH

herb sprigs

PREPARATION TIME
20 minutes
FREEZING
Not suitable

285 CALS PER SERVING

1. Carefully wash all the salad ingredients and allow to drain in a colander. Tear the leaves into smaller pieces if necessary and place in a salad bowl.

2. Peel the carrot and cut into fine julienne strips. Cut the fennel, celery and courgette into batons. Leave the cherry tomatoes whole. Slice the chicory. Slice the red onion very finely. Add these ingredients to the salad leaves and toss lightly.

3. To make the dressing, place the oil, vinegar, mustard, sugar and seasoning in a screw-topped jar and shake vigorously to combine. Add the herbs to the dressing just prior to serving.

4. To serve, pour the dressing over the salad and toss lightly. Serve at once, garnished with herb sprigs. A flavoured bread – such as olive or walnut – is an ideal accompaniement for mopping up the juices.

NOTE: For this salad, the usual practice of carefully patting the leaves dry with kitchen paper doesn't apply. Any water clinging to the leaves after washing blends with the dressing.

VARIATIONS

For added interest, add a sprinkling of sesame or pumpkin seeds. Alternatively include a handful of roughly chopped pecans, hazelnuts, cashews or walnuts for added crunch.

TECHNIQUE

Cut the carrot into julienne strips. Slice the courgettes, fennel and celery into batons.

APRICOT AND CASHEW NUT SALAD

This is a quick and easy salad to prepare. Dried apricots are soaked in white wine, then tossed with a selection of bitter leaves, carrot and pepper julienne, and chopped coriander. Roasted salted cashews add a delicious crunch. You can of course use any combination of leaves.

SERVES 4-6

125 g (4 oz) dried apricots

150 ml (¼ pint) dry white
  wine, such as Chardonnay

1 head of chicory

50 g (2 oz) watercress

25 g (1 oz) rocket leaves

handful of young spinach
  leaves

1 small carrot

½ medium green pepper

50-75 g (2-3 oz) roasted
  salted cashew nuts

15 ml (1 tbsp) chopped fresh
  coriander

DRESSING

reserved wine from soaking
  apricots

60 ml (4 tbsp) extra-virgin
  olive oil

30 ml (2 tbsp) orange juice
  (freshly squeezed)

5 ml (1 tsp) clear honey

coarse sea salt and pepper

PREPARATION TIME
10-15 minutes, plus soaking
COOKING TIME
Nil
FREEZING
Not suitable

345-230 CALS PER SERVING

1. Cut the apricots into slices, using a sharp knife or scissors. Place in a bowl and pour over the wine. Leave to soak for 2 hours.

2. Meanwhile prepare the salad. Separate the chicory leaves. Wash all the salad leaves and carefully pat dry with kitchen paper. Peel the carrot and cut into julienne strips. Remove the core and seeds from the green pepper and slice thinly. Pick over the watercress, removing any discoloured leaves or tough stalks. Combine all of the salad leaves and vegetables in a salad bowl.

3. To make the dressing, drain the wine from the apricots into a screw-topped jar. Add the olive oil, orange juice, honey and seasoning. Shake well to combine.

4. Add the apricots, cashew nuts and chopped coriander to the salad and toss lightly. Drizzle over some of the dressing; serve the remainder separately.

TECHNIQUE

Wash the salad leaves in a colander under cold running water.

VARIATION

Replace the apricots with dried pears, and the cashew nuts with pecans. Add 1.25 ml (¼ tsp) French mustard to the dressing.

SPICED COLESLAW WITH PECANS

This is a hot version of the ever-popular coleslaw – the difference being that the ingredients are tossed in a chilli-flavoured mayonnaise. For added interest, I have included pecans and celery. If possible make this salad the day before, or at least several hours ahead, to enable the flavours of the dressing to be absorbed. Serve with a jacket potato for a tasty lunch or supper.

SERVES 4

350 g (12 oz) white cabbage
225 g (8 oz) carrots
2-3 celery sticks
50 g (2 oz) pecans or
  walnuts (optional)
DRESSING
75 ml (5 tbsp) mayonnaise
30 ml (2 tbsp) olive oil
30 ml (2 tbsp) wine vinegar
5 ml (1 tsp) chilli powder
10 ml (2 tsp) mango chutney
  (optional)
4 drops of Tabasco sauce
coarse sea salt and pepper
TO GARNISH
paprika, for sprinkling
chervil or parsley sprigs

PREPARATION TIME
15 minutes, plus standing
COOKING TIME
Nil
FREEZING
Not suitable

340 CALS PER SERVING

1. Remove the core from the cabbage and slice finely. Peel the carrots and grate coarsely, using a grating disc in a food processor, or by hand. Finely slice the celery. Combine the cabbage, carrots and celery in a large bowl.

2. To make the dressing, put all of the ingredients into a screw-topped jar and shake vigorously to combine.

3. Pour the dressing over the salad and toss well. Cover and leave to stand for several hours or overnight if possible, in a cool place.

4. Just before serving, toss the pecans into the salad. Sprinkle with a little paprika and garnish with chervil or parsley.

VARIATION

To make the dressing suitable for vegans, substitute 125 g (4 oz) tofu for the mayonnaise. Put all of the dressing ingredients into a blender or food processor and work until smooth, adding a little more oil to thin if necessary.

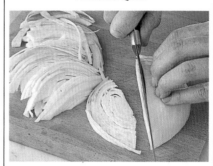

TECHNIQUE

Cut the cabbage into fine slices, using a sharp knife.

YELLOW PEPPER CAESAR SALAD

This version of Caesar Salad has huge hot, buttery croûtons and, in contrast, delicate slivers of smoky grilled yellow pepper. Both are tossed into crisp lettuce leaves and dressed with garlic and Parmesan flavoured mayonnaise. It's important to assemble the salad at the last minute when the croûtons are fresh from the oven.

SERVES 4-6

3 large yellow peppers
1 cos lettuce
25 g (1 oz) finely pared
   Parmesan cheese
DRESSING
75 ml (5 tbsp) mayonnaise
1-2 garlic cloves
coarse sea salt and pepper
45 ml (3 tbsp) finely grated
   Parmesan cheese
CROUTONS
1 small rustic white loaf
   (uncut)
75 g (3 oz) butter

PREPARATION TIME
20 minutes
COOKING TIME
20-30 minutes
FREEZING
Not suitable

505-340 CALS PER SERVING

1. First make the dressing: Put the mayonnaise in a bowl and stir in 45-60 ml (3-4 tbsp) water to thin to a pouring consistency. Peel the garlic cloves and crush to a paste on a chopping board with a little coarse sea salt. Add to the mayonnaise with the Parmesan and stir well. Thin the dressing with a little more water if necessary to keep it pourable. Season with pepper and set aside.

2. Preheat the grill to high. Cut the peppers in half lengthwise and remove the seeds. Grill the pepper halves, skin side up, for 10-15 minutes until the skin is blistered and blackened. Cover and leave to cool slightly, then peel off and discard the charred skin. Cut the peppers into long, thin strips.

3. Preheat the oven to 200°C (400°F) Mark 6.

4. Meanwhile, separate the lettuce leaves, wash and shake dry. Tear into large pieces and place in a large shallow salad bowl. Add the yellow pepper strips and set aside.

5. To make the croûtons, cut the bread into 3 cm (1¼ inch) thick slices. Cut off the crusts and discard, along with the end pieces. Melt the butter in a small saucepan and use a brush to butter the slices of bread on all sides. Cut the bread into 3 cm (1¼ inch) cubes.

6. Brush a large flat baking dish with a little butter. Arrange the bread cubes on it in a single layer, brushing the cut sides with any remaining butter. Bake in the preheated oven for about 12 minutes until crisp and deep golden brown; check the croûtons frequently after 8 minutes because they tend to change colour suddenly towards the end of cooking.

7. Tip the piping hot croûtons into the salad, drizzle over the dressing and sprinkle the Parmesan slivers over the top. Serve at once.

TECHNIQUE

Grilling the peppers until they are well charred ensures that the skins can be peeled away easily, when cool enough to handle.

POTATO SALAD WITH CELERY, WALNUTS AND BLUE CHEESE

In this warm, tasty salad, the earthy flavour of potato is perfectly complemented by celery, walnuts and blue cheese. The warmth of the cooked potatoes marries the flavours together and melts the blue cheese slightly. It is important to serve the salad immediately, in a warmed dish.

SERVES 4-6

450 g (1 lb) new potatoes
2 garlic cloves (see note)
coarse sea salt and pepper
60 ml (4 tbsp) walnut oil
125 g (4 oz) walnuts
1 celery heart
125 g (4 oz) vegetarian blue
   Stilton cheese
TO GARNISH
thyme sprigs
celery leaves (optional)

PREPARATION TIME
10 minutes
COOKING TIME
15-20 minutes
FREEZING
Not suitable

560-370 CALS PER SERVING

1. Scrub the potatoes clean; cut any larger ones in half. Cook in boiling salted water for 15-20 minutes depending on size, until tender.

2. Meanwhile, peel the garlic and crush with a little salt, using a pestle and mortar. Add the walnut oil and half of the walnuts and work to a thick sauce. Alternatively put the garlic, salt, oil and half of the walnuts in a food processor or blender and whizz to combine.

3. Roughly chop the remaining walnuts. Crumble the cheese into small pieces. Thinly slice the celery, reserving some leaves for garnish if available.

4. When the potatoes are cooked, drain thoroughly and turn into a warmed serving bowl. Immediately add the dressing, celery, remaining walnuts and crumbled cheese and toss lightly. Garnish with thyme, and celery leaves if available, and serve immediately, while the potatoes are still warm and the cheese is melting slightly.

NOTE: If smoked garlic is available, use it for this salad – it will impart a delicious smoky flavour.

VARIATION

Substitute roasted hazelnuts and hazelnut oil for the walnuts and walnut oil.

TECHNIQUE

Use a pestle and mortar to mix the garlic, salt, walnut oil and half of the walnuts to a thick sauce.

MEDITERRANEAN PASTA SALAD

The flavours of the Mediterranean are captured in this salad of pasta, sun-dried tomatoes, black olives, basil leaves, shredded spring onions and cherry tomatoes. Any pasta shapes can be used: if preferred use *tricolore* pasta – a mixture of spinach, tomato and plain pasta.

SERVES 4

175 g (6 oz) fresh or dried pasta shapes

30 ml (2 tbsp) extra-virgin olive oil

4 sun-dried tomatoes in oil, drained

4-6 spring onions

225 g (8 oz) cherry tomatoes

about 8-12 black olives

8-12 basil leaves

DRESSING

2 sun-dried tomatoes in oil, drained

30 ml (2 tbsp) oil (from the sun-dried tomato jar)

30 ml (2 tbsp) red wine vinegar

1 garlic clove

15 ml (1 tbsp) tomato purée

pinch of sugar (optional)

coarse sea salt and pepper

30 ml (2 tbsp) extra-virgin olive oil

PREPARATION TIME
15 minutes, plus standing
COOKING TIME
2-10 minutes
FREEZING
Not suitable

415 CALS PER SERVING

1. Cook the pasta in a large pan of boiling salted water with 15 ml (1 tbsp) olive oil added until *al dente*, just tender but still firm to the bite. Fresh pasta will only take about 2-3 minutes; for dried pasta refer to the packet instructions. Drain the pasta in a colander, then refresh under cold running water. Drain thoroughly and transfer to a large bowl. Stir in 15 ml (1 tbsp) olive oil to prevent the pasta from sticking together.

2. Slice the sun-dried tomatoes. Trim and finely shred the spring onions. Halve the cherry tomatoes. Tear the basil leaves into smaller pieces, if preferred.

3. Add the sun-dried and cherry tomatoes, spring onions, olives and basil to the pasta and toss to mix.

4. To make the dressing, put the sun-dried tomatoes (with their oil), vinegar, garlic and tomato purée in a blender or food processor. Add the sugar if using, and salt and pepper. With the motor running, pour the oil through the feeder tube and process briefly to make a fairly thick dressing.

5. Pour the dressing over the pasta and toss well. Cover and leave to stand to allow the flavours to mingle for 1-2 hours before serving if possible.

NOTE: Take extra care to avoid overcooking the pasta and quickly cool it under cold running water to preserve the texture.

VARIATION

Toss cubes of mature vegetarian Cheddar into the salad and serve with wholemeal bread and a leafy green salad for a main course.

TECHNIQUE

Finely shred the spring onions lengthwise, using a sharp knife.

BULGAR WHEAT SALAD WITH FETA AND HERBS

Bulgar wheat is a nutritious type of cracked wheat with a slightly nutty flavour. It readily absorbs the flavours of the lemony herb dressing in this colourful salad and marries perfectly with the cucumber, tomatoes, peppers and feta cheese. Toasted hazelnuts add a delicious crunch.

SERVES 6-8

225 g (8 oz) bulgar wheat
½ cucumber
salt and pepper
½ green pepper
½ red pepper
1 bunch of spring onions
2-3 tomatoes
125 g (4 oz) feta cheese,
  diced
DRESSING
60 ml (4 tbsp) extra-virgin
  olive oil
45 ml (3 tbsp) lemon juice
1 garlic clove, crushed
30 ml (2 tbsp) chopped fresh
  mint
30 ml (2 tbsp) chopped fresh
  parsley
TO SERVE
125 g (4 oz) hazelnuts,
  skinned
herb sprigs, to garnish

PREPARATION TIME
20 minutes, plus standing
COOKING TIME
1 minute
FREEZING
Not suitable

430-325 CALS PER SERVING

1. Put the bulgar wheat in a bowl and pour on 300 ml (½ pint) boiling water. Leave to soak for 30 minutes or until the water has been absorbed, stirring occasionally.

2. Meanwhile, roughly chop the cucumber, sprinkle with salt and leave for 15 minutes. Rinse thoroughly, drain and pat dry.

3. Remove the core and seeds from the peppers, then cut into strips. Blanch in boiling water for 1 minute, then drain. Trim the spring onions and slice diagonally. Slice the tomatoes.

4. If necessary, drain the bulgar wheat, then place in a large bowl. Add the cucumber, peppers, spring onions, tomatoes and feta cheese.

5. To make the dressing, in a bowl whisk together the olive oil, lemon juice, garlic and seasoning. Pour over the salad and add the mint and parsley. Toss lightly and refrigerate until required.

6. Toast the hazelnuts under a preheated grill until evenly browned.

7. Serve the salad on individual plates, sprinkled with the hazelnuts and garnished with herbs.

VARIATION

Instead of bulgar wheat, use 175 g (6 oz) long-grain white rice and 50 g (2 oz) wild rice. Cook according to packet directions, then drain and refresh under cold running water.

TECHNIQUE

Soak the bulgar wheat in boiling water for 30 minutes, stirring occasionally to separate the grains.

BAKED VEGETABLES WITH A SPICY SAUCE

A colourful selection of vegetables are marinated in olive oil flavoured with rosemary, then baked until crisp and browned. Served with a spicy sauce, and some crusty bread for mopping up the juices, they make a tasty main course. Vary the vegetables according to whatever is available.

SERVES 4-6

1 red pepper
1 yellow or orange pepper
6 shallots
1 aubergine
2-3 courgettes
1 fennel bulb
175 g (6 oz) parsnips
125 g (4 oz) baby corn cobs
6-8 cherry tomatoes
225 g (8 oz) mushrooms
   (large closed cup)
2-3 rosemary sprigs
120 ml (4 fl oz) extra-virgin
   olive oil
coarse sea salt and pepper
SPICY SAUCE:
1 small onion
1 garlic clove
1 green chilli
15 ml (1 tbsp) sunflower oil
10 ml (2 tsp) capers
10 ml (2 tsp) soft brown sugar
juice of ½ lemon
175 g (6 oz) passata

PREPARATION TIME
30 minutes, plus standing
COOKING TIME
40 minutes
FREEZING
Not suitable

425-285 CALS PER SERVING

1. First prepare the vegetables. Halve the peppers, then remove the core and seeds. Peel the shallots and leave whole. Cut the aubergine into thin slices. Thickly slice the courgettes on the diagonal. Quarter the fennel bulb lengthwise. Halve or quarter the parsnips. Halve the baby corn lengthwise. Cut a shallow cross on the base of each tomato, but leave them whole. Wipe the mushrooms with a damp cloth and leave whole.

2. Strip the leaves from one of the rosemary sprigs and chop finely to release their fragrance. Pour the olive oil into a large bowl and add the chopped rosemary and whole sprigs with salt and pepper. Add the vegetables and turn carefully with a spoon to coat evenly with the oil. Leave to infuse for 1-2 hours, or longer if time.

3. Preheat the oven to 220°C (425°F) Mark 7.

4. Put all of the vegetables, except the cherry tomatoes, into a large shallow baking tin with the rosemary sprigs and baste with the oil. Cook, turning and basting from time to time, for about 40 minutes until the vegetables are evenly browned and cooked through. Add the cherry tomatoes 10 minutes from the end of the cooking time.

5. To make the sauce, peel and finely slice the onion and garlic. Halve the chilli, remove the seeds and slice finely. Heat the oil in a small pan, add the onion, garlic and chilli and fry gently until tender.

6. Meanwhile put the capers, sugar, lemon juice and passata in a blender or food processor and work until smooth. Season with salt and pepper and add to the chilli mixture. Cover and cook for 5-10 minutes, stirring occasionally, to make a thick sauce. If a thinner sauce is preferred, dilute with a little water. Pour the sauce into a warm serving jug.

7. Transfer the baked vegetables to an oval serving platter and serve at once, accompanied by the sauce.

TECHNIQUE

Toss the vegetables in the rosemary oil and allow to marinate before baking.

36

ROAST PEPPERS STUFFED WITH MUSHROOMS

Sweet peppers are partially roasted before stuffing to give them a delicious smoky flavour. The skin may be removed if preferred at this stage, but the peppers will not hold their shape so well. I like to serve the peppers accompanied by tomato-flavoured bread (see below) or warm crusty bread and a leafy green salad.

SERVES 4

2 large orange or red
    peppers
2 large yellow peppers
FILLING
450 g (I lb) tomatoes, or a
    400 g (14 oz) can chopped
    tomatoes
I large onion
2-3 garlic cloves
45 ml (3 tbsp) extra-virgin
    olive oil
30 ml (2 tbsp) tomato purée
5 ml (I tsp) light muscovado
    sugar
salt and pepper
50 g (2 oz) mushrooms
50 g (2 oz) pine nuts or
    flaked almonds
15 ml (I tbsp) fresh marjoram
    leaves, roughly torn
50 g (2 oz) black olives
25-50 g (1-2 oz) freshly
    grated Parmesan cheese

PREPARATION TIME
20 minutes
COOKING TIME
30-35 minutes
FREEZING
Not suitable

315 CALS PER SERVING

1. Preheat the oven to 200°C (400°F) Mark 6. Halve the peppers lengthwise, then remove the core and seeds. Place cut-side down on a baking sheet and roast in the oven for 15 minutes, turning frequently. Place the peppers, cut side up, in an ovenproof dish.

2. Meanwhile make the sauce. If using fresh tomatoes, place in a bowl, add boiling water to cover and leave for 15-30 seconds. Transfer to a bowl of cold water to cool, then remove and peel away the skins. Roughly chop the tomatoes.

3. Peel and finely chop the onion and garlic. Heat 30 ml (2 tbsp) of the oil in a saucepan, add the onion and garlic and fry gently until softened and lightly coloured. Add the tomatoes, tomato purée, sugar, salt and pepper. Cook, uncovered, for 15-20 minutes until reduced to a thick sauce. Check the seasoning.

4. Meanwhile, wipe the mushrooms over with a damp cloth and slice thickly. Heat the remaining 15 ml (I tbsp) oil in a pan and sauté the mushroom slices until softened.

5. Place the peppers, cut-side up, in an ovenproof dish. Transfer two thirds of the tomato mixture to a bowl and stir in the mushrooms, nuts, marjoram and

olives. Fill the peppers with the mixture and top with the grated Parmesan cheese. Bake in the oven for 15-20 minutes until thoroughly heated through.

6. Serve one red pepper half and one yellow pepper half per person, accompanied by plenty of crusty bread or baked tomato and sesame bread (see note), and a simple green salad.

NOTE: Use any remaining sauce to make a tasty accompaniment. Spread thick slices of crusty bread with the tomato mixture and sprinkle with sesame seeds. Warm through in the oven.

TECHNIQUE

Spoon the tomato and mushroom filling into the pepper halves, dividing it equally between them.

SPINACH TAGLIATELLE WITH BLUE CHEESE

This tasty main course can be prepared and cooked in a matter of minutes. If you happen to have a local Italian delicatessen which sells freshly made pasta, do use it for this recipe, otherwise dried pasta is fine. Serve as soon as it is ready, accompanied by a mixed salad.

SERVES 4

4-6 spring onions
400 g (14 oz) fresh or dried
   spinach tagliatelle
150 g (5 oz) ricotta cheese
150 g (5 oz) vegetarian blue
   Stilton cheese
150 g (5 oz) crème fraîche
15 ml (1 tbsp) chopped fresh
   coriander leaves
coarse sea salt and pepper
TO GARNISH
coriander sprigs

PREPARATION TIME
5 minutes
COOKING TIME
2-12 minutes
FREEZING
Not suitable

695 CALS PER SERVING

1. Trim the spring onions and finely chop them.

2. Cook the tagliatelle in a large pan of boiling salted water, until *al dente*, tender but still firm to the bite. The worst thing you can do to pasta is to overcook it, so be careful! Fresh pasta will only take 2-3 minutes to cook; for dried pasta, refer to the packet instructions.

3. While the pasta is cooking, crumble the ricotta and Stilton cheeses together into a bowl. Add the crème fraîche and stir to mix well.

4. Drain the pasta thoroughly in a colander and turn into a heated serving dish. Immediately add the crumbled cheese mixture, spring onions and chopped coriander leaves. Using two forks, lift the tagliatelle to coat with the sauce. Garnish with sprigs of coriander and serve immediately.

VARIATION

Replace the spring onions with 225 g (8 oz) leeks. Clean the leeks thoroughly then slice. Sauté in a little olive oil until softened. Add to the pasta with the crumbled cheese mixture and toss well.

TECHNIQUE

Drain the pasta thoroughly in a colander as soon as it is cooked.

BAKED BLACK-EYED BEAN CASSEROLE

As a child I thought baked beans always came out of a tin until friends returning from living in America introduced me to Boston baked beans. The marvel of how different they were is still with me to this day, and this vegetarian version is modified from their recipe. Serve with garlic bread or jacket potatoes, and accompanied by a crisp, colourful salad.

SERVES 4

**225 g (8 oz) black-eyed
  beans**
1 large garlic clove
1 large onion
30 ml (2 tbsp) olive oil
600 ml (1 pint) dry cider
150 ml (¼ pint) passata
30 ml (2 tbsp) tomato purée
15 ml (1 tbsp) black treacle
**15 ml (1 tbsp) demerara
  sugar**
5 ml (1 tsp) French mustard
coarse sea salt and pepper
TO GARNISH
parsley sprigs

PREPARATION TIME
10 minutes, plus overnight
soaking
COOKING TIME
2-2½ hours
FREEZING
Not suitable

345 CALS PER SERVING

1. Soak the black-eyed beans overnight in plenty of cold water.

2. Drain the beans, rinse thoroughly and place in a large saucepan. Cover with plenty of fresh cold water, bring to the boil and boil steadily for 10 minutes. Remove any scum with a slotted spoon. Lower the heat, cover and simmer for a further 20 minutes. Do not add seasoning at this stage as it toughens the beans. Drain the beans.

3. Preheat the oven to 170°C (325°F) Mark 3. Peel and finely chop the garlic. Peel and chop the onion.

4. Heat the oil in a saucepan, add the onion and garlic and fry gently until tender. Add the cider, passata, tomato purée, black treacle, sugar and mustard. Bring to the boil.

5. Transfer the black-eyed beans to a casserole and add the prepared sauce. Stir well until evenly mixed, then cover and cook in the oven for 1½-2 hours or until the beans are tender. Check and stir the beans occasionally during cooking and add a little extra cider or water if necessary to prevent them drying out; the finished sauce should be thick and syrupy. Season with salt and pepper to taste.

6. Garnish with parsley and serve with hot crusty garlic bread or jacket potatoes and a salad.

NOTE: The cooking time for pulses varies considerably. The longer the beans have been stored, the longer they will take to cook.

VARIATION

Instead of black-eyed beans, use haricot beans or another pulse variety, adjusting the cooking time accordingly.

TECHNIQUE

Turn the partially cooked beans in the sauce to mix thoroughly.

ROOT VEGETABLE AND LENTIL CASSEROLE

This spicy combination of mixed root vegetables and assorted lentils makes an ideal winter supper dish. Serve it with plenty of warm crusty bread and a side salad or seasonal green vegetable, such as broccoli or spinach.

SERVES 6

5 ml (1 tsp) cumin seeds

15 ml (1 tbsp) coriander
  seeds

5 ml (1 tsp) mustard seeds

25 g (1 oz) fresh root ginger

3 onions

450 g (1 lb) carrots

350 g (12 oz) leeks

350 g (12 oz) mooli (white
  radish)

450 g (1 lb) button
  mushrooms

45 ml (3 tbsp) olive oil

2 garlic cloves, crushed

1.25 ml (¼ tsp) turmeric

175 g (6 oz) split red lentils

50 g (2 oz) brown or green
  lentils

salt and pepper

30 ml (2 tbsp) chopped
  coriander leaves (optional)

TO GARNISH

parsley sprigs

PREPARATION TIME
20 minutes
COOKING TIME
About 1 hour
FREEZING
Not suitable

260 CALS PER SERVING

1. Preheat the oven to 180°C (350°F) Mark 4. Crush the cumin, coriander and mustard seeds in a mortar with a pestle (or in a strong bowl with the end of a rolling pin). Peel and grate or finely chop the ginger.

2. Peel and slice the onions and carrots. Clean the leeks thoroughly, then cut into slices. Peel and roughly chop the mooli; halve the mushrooms if large.

3. Heat the oil in a large flameproof casserole. Add the onions, carrots, leeks and mooli, and fry for 2-3 minutes, stirring constantly. Add the mushrooms, garlic, ginger, turmeric and crushed spices, and fry for a further 2-3 minutes, stirring.

4. Rinse the lentils in a colander under cold running water, then drain. Stir the lentils into the casserole with 750 ml (1¼ pints) boiling water. Season with salt and pepper and return to the boil. Cover and cook in the oven for about 45 minutes or until the vegetables and lentils are tender. Stir in the coriander if using, and adjust the seasoning before serving, garnished with parsley.

VARIATION

Replace the mooli (white radish) with parsnips or young turnips.

TECHNIQUE

Use a pestle and mortar to crush the cumin, coriander and mustard seeds.

VEGETABLE COUSCOUS

For this quick tasty version of the famous Moroccan dish, couscous grains are steamed over a nourishing spicy vegetable stew. Use quick-cook couscous – which needs to be moistened before cooking but doesn't require lengthy soaking. Vary the vegetables as you like.

SERVES 4

225 g (8 oz) quick-cook couscous
225 g (8 oz) aubergine
175 g (6 oz) courgettes
175 g (6 oz) carrots, peeled
1 large onion, peeled
15 ml (1 tbsp) oil
2 garlic cloves, crushed
10 ml (2 tsp) ground cumin
2.5 ml (½ tsp) mild chilli seasoning
2.5 ml (½ tsp) ground ginger
60 ml (4 tbsp) tomato purée
1 bay leaf
175 g (6 oz) canned chick peas drained, or frozen broad beans
750 ml (1¼ pints) vegetable stock
salt and pepper
TO GARNISH
chopped parsley
paprika (optional)

PREPARATION TIME
15 minutes
COOKING TIME
15 minutes
FREEZING
Not suitable

260 CALS PER SERVING

1. Moisten the couscous according to the packet instructions. Cut the aubergine and courgettes into chunks. Chop the carrots. Finely chop the onion. Heat the oil in a saucepan (over which a steamer, metal sieve or colander will fit). Add the onion, carrots, garlic and spices and cook gently for 1 minute, stirring occasionally.

2. Add the tomato purée, bay leaf, aubergine, courgettes and chick peas or broad beans. Stir in the stock. Cover and bring to the boil, then uncover and boil rapidly for 8 minutes.

3. Meanwhile, fork the couscous to break up any lumps and spread in a steamer, metal sieve or colander lined with a double thickness of muslin.

4. Place the couscous container over the cooking vegetables. Cover and cook for 5 minutes or until the vegetables are tender, the sauce is well reduced and the couscous is piping hot. Check the seasoning.

5. Spoon the couscous onto a warmed serving dish and fork through. Pile the vegetables and juices on top. Garnish with plenty of chopped parsley and sprinkle with paprika to serve if desired.

VARIATION

Replace the tomato purée with 350 g (12 oz) fresh tomatoes, skinned and quartered. Include other vegetables, such as cauliflower florets, sliced leeks and diced red pepper.

TECHNIQUE

Moisten the couscous grains with warm water, according to packet instructions.

SUMMER VEGETABLE FLAN

Young, tender baby vegetables are set in a creamy cheese filling well flavoured with herbs, and baked in a crisp walnut pastry crust. You can use any selection of summer vegetables – just be sure to blanch or sauté them first and keep the total amount to about 700 g (1½ lb).

SERVES 6

WALNUT PASTRY
50 g (2 oz) walnut pieces
175 g (6 oz) plain flour
pinch of salt
125 g (4 oz) vegetable
 margarine or butter
FILLING
1 garlic clove
175 g (6 oz) courgettes
25 g (1 oz) vegetable
 margarine or butter
175 g (6 oz) broccoli florets
 or baby carrots
175 g (6 oz) thin asparagus
50 g (2 oz) peas
125 g (4 oz) tomatoes
50 g (2 oz) sun-dried
 tomatoes in oil, drained
125 g (4 oz) full-fat soft
 cheese
150 ml (¼ pint) single cream
2 whole eggs, plus 1 egg yolk
30 ml (2 tbsp) chopped fresh
 mixed herbs
salt and pepper
40 g (1½ oz) vegetarian
 mature Cheddar cheese

PREPARATION TIME
40 minutes
COOKING TIME
About 1 hour
FREEZING
Suitable: Baked pastry case only

520 CALS PER SERVING

1. To prepare the nut pastry, spread the walnut pieces on a baking sheet and grill until golden, turning frequently. Allow to cool, then grind to a powder in a blender or food processor.

2. Sift the flour and salt into a bowl and stir in the ground walnuts. Rub in the margarine or butter until the mixture resembles fine breadcrumbs. Using a round-bladed knife, mix in sufficient water to bind the pastry; you will need about 45 ml (3 tbsp). Wrap the pastry in greaseproof paper or cling film and chill in the refrigerator for 30 minutes.

3. Roll out the pastry on a lightly floured surface and use to line a 3 cm (1¼ inch) deep, 23 cm (9 inch) loose-based, fluted flan tin. Prick the base of the flan with a fork and chill for 30 minutes.

4. Preheat the oven to 200°C (400°F) Mark 6. Line the flan case with grease-proof paper and baking beans and bake blind in the oven for 20 minutes or until set, removing the paper and beans for the last 5 minutes. Lower the oven temperature to 180°C (350°F) Mark 4.

5. Meanwhile, prepare the filling. Peel and thinly slice the garlic. Thinly slice the courgettes. Heat the margarine or butter in a pan and sauté the courgettes with the garlic until golden.

6. Peel the carrots (if using) and trim

the broccoli and asparagus. Blanch the carrots, asparagus and peas in boiling salted water for 1-2 minutes. Drain thoroughly. Cut the fresh and sun-dried tomatoes into quarters.

7. Put the soft cheese in a bowl and gradually beat in the cream. Add the eggs, egg yolk, herbs and seasoning, mixing well.

8. Pile all the vegetables into the flan case and pour the cream mixture around them; the vegetables should protrude above the sauce. Grate the cheese over the top. Bake in the oven for 35-40 minutes or until just set. Allow to stand for about 15 minutes before serving warm.

TECHNIQUE

Line the pastry case with greaseproof paper and baking beans to bake blind.

VEGETABLE CURRY

It is well worth mixing your own spices for this Indian curry. If possible buy whole spices and grind them yourself, using a pestle and mortar or an electric grinder. You will find that the flavour is infinitely better than if you use commercially prepared curry powder. Vary the vegetables according to whatever is available.

SERVES 4-6

1.4 kg (3 lb) mixed vegetables, including cauliflower, carrots, potato, parsnip and frozen peas

1 medium onion

2.5 cm (1 inch) piece of fresh root ginger

2 green chillies

1-2 garlic cloves, peeled

30 ml (2 tbsp) vegetable ghee or oil

10 ml (2 tsp) ground turmeric

10 ml (2 tsp) ground coriander

10 ml (2 tsp) ground cumin

5 ml (1 tsp) ground fenugreek

8 whole cloves

8 green cardamom pods

1 cinnamon stick

600 ml (1 pint) coconut milk

salt and pepper

TO GARNISH

coriander sprigs

PREPARATION TIME
20 minutes
COOKING TIME
About 1 hour
FREEZING
Suitable

685-445 CALS PER SERVING

1. First prepare the vegetables. Divide the cauliflower into florets. Peel the carrots, potato and parsnip and cut into chunks.

2. Peel and chop the onion and ginger. Halve the chillies and remove the seeds. Put the onion, ginger, garlic and chillies in a blender or food processor and purée until almost smooth.

3. Heat the ghee or oil in a large heavy-based saucepan, add the onion mixture and fry for 5 minutes, stirring constantly. Add all the spices and cook over a high heat for 3-4 minutes, stirring all the time.

4. Add the vegetables to the pan and stir to coat in the spice paste. Gradually stir in the coconut milk and 300 ml (½ pint) water. Bring to the boil, then lower the heat, cover and simmer for 45-55 minutes or until the vegetables are just tender, depending on the type of vegetables used. Season with salt and pepper to taste. Leave the curry to stand for 5 minutes to let the flavours develop before serving, garnished with coriander sprigs. Accompany with naan bread, pickles and plain boiled rice.

NOTE: If canned coconut milk is not available use one 225 g (8 oz) block of creamed coconut or 100 g (3.5 oz) packet of instant coconut milk powder with 600 ml (1 pint) boiling water.

TECHNIQUE

Purée the onion, ginger, garlic and chillies to a paste in a food processor or blender.

TOMATO AND GARLIC PIZZA

This thin, crispy pizza has a delicious topping of flavourful fresh tomatoes, black olives, garlic cloves and feta cheese. On baking the garlic loses its pungency and becomes deliciously soft with a mild, nutty flavour.

SERVES 2

1 medium garlic bulb
olive oil, for basting
4 medium tomatoes, about
   400 g (14 oz)
salt and pepper
145 g (5.1 oz) packet pizza-
   base mix
15 ml (1 tbsp) chopped fresh
   rosemary or 10 ml (2 tsp)
   dried
75 g (3 oz) feta cheese
about 8 black olives
about 8 fresh basil leaves

PREPARATION TIME
15 minutes
COOKING TIME
20 minutes
FREEZING
Not suitable

485 CALS PER SERVING

1. Preheat the oven to 220°C (425°F) Mark 7. Divide the garlic into cloves, discarding the outer, papery layers, but leaving the inner skins intact. Toss in a little oil.

2. Meanwhile, roughly chop the tomatoes and place in a bowl with 5 ml (1 tsp) salt. Mix well.

3. Make up the pizza base mix according to the packet instructions. As you are kneading the dough, knead in the rosemary until it is evenly incorporated.

4. Roll out the dough thinly to a 25 cm (10 inch) round on a lightly floured surface. Transfer to a lightly greased and floured baking sheet.

5. Spoon the tomatoes over the pizza base to within 1 cm (½ inch) of the edge and crumble the feta cheese on top. Scatter the olives, garlic cloves and basil over the top. Season with pepper only.

6. Bake in the oven for 20 minutes or until the base is crisp and golden. Serve immediately, mashing down the garlic cloves as you eat.

NOTE: For this recipe the pizza dough is rolled out to a larger round than suggested on the packet instructions to give a thin, crispy result.

VARIATION

Replace the garlic, olives and feta cheese with a 340 g (12 oz) jar of pimientos, drained; 20 ml (4 tsp) capers; and 75 g (3 oz) smoked Vegetarian cheese.

TECHNIQUE

Roll out the pizza dough to a 25 cm (10 inch) round on a lightly floured surface.

MUSHROOM AND PARMESAN RISOTTO

This is a wonderfully warming meal for a cold night. If possible, use the Italian risotto rice – Arborio – which has the capacity to absorb plenty of liquid during cooking without turning mushy. Make sure you pare the lemon rind in one large piece, so it's easy to remove.

SERVES 4

1 medium onion
1 lemon
175 g (6 oz) flat mushrooms
225 g (8 oz) broccoli florets
175 g (6 oz) French beans
salt and pepper
30 ml (2 tbsp) olive oil
350 g (12 oz) Arborio
   (risotto) or long-grain
   white rice (see note)
pinch of saffron threads
   (optional)
60 ml (4 tbsp) dry white
   wine
750 ml (1¼ pints) vegetable
   stock
TO SERVE
finely pared Parmesan
   cheese

PREPARATION TIME
15 minutes
COOKING TIME
20 minutes
FREEZING
Not suitable

420 CALS PER SERVING

1. Peel and finely chop the onion. Finely pare the rind from the lemon, using a vegetable peeler, then squeeze the juice. Wipe the mushrooms clean with a damp cloth, then slice.

2. Break the broccoli into small florets. Top and tail the French beans and cut in half lengthways. Blanch the broccoli and beans together in boiling salted water for 3-4 minutes. Drain and refresh under cold running water.

3. Heat the oil in a heavy-based saucepan or flameproof casserole, and cook the onion gently for about 2-3 minutes until beginning to soften. Stir in the rice and saffron, if using. Season well and pour in the wine. Add the pared lemon rind, 30 ml (2 tbsp) lemon juice and the stock. Bring to the boil, stirring.

4. Cover and simmer the risotto for 5 minutes. Stir in the mushrooms, broccoli and French beans. Re-cover and simmer for a further 5 minutes, or until the rice is tender and most of the liquid is absorbed.

5. Discard the lemon rind and transfer the risotto to warmed serving plates. Top with slivers of Parmesan cheese and serve at once.

NOTE: If you use Arborio rice you may need to add a little more stock and cook the risotto for 1-2 minutes longer.

VARIATION

Replace the broccoli and French beans with 400 g (14 oz) fine asparagus, trimmed and halved.

TECHNIQUE

After 5 minutes, gently stir in the mushrooms, broccoli and French beans.

MIXED ONION CASSEROLE WITH JUNIPER

This delicious casserole is baked slowly in the oven until the onions are partly caramelised and acquire a sweet, mellow flavour. Serve as a tasty accompaniment to a savoury pie or bake. Alternatively, serve with a jacket potato and green beans as a substantial supper dish in its own right.

SERVES 4

6 medium onions
1 bunch of spring onions
6-8 shallots
5 garlic cloves
8 juniper berries
50 g (2 oz) butter
600 ml (1 pint) vegetable
 stock (approximately)
coarse sea salt and pepper
6 slices French bread, 1 cm
 (½ inch) thick
125 g (4 oz) coarsely grated
 vegetarian mature
 Cheddar cheese
TO GARNISH
15 ml (1 tbsp) snipped
 chives

PREPARATION TIME
15 minutes
COOKING TIME
1½ hours
FREEZING
Not suitable

460 CALS PER SERVING

1. Preheat the oven to 180°C (350°F) Mark 4.

2. Peel four of the onions, taking care to trim the minimum from the tops and bases. Cut each one crosswise into quarters, leaving the root end intact to ensure the onions do not fall apart during cooking.

3. Peel, halve and slice the remaining ordinary onions. Trim the spring onions, then slice both the white and green parts. Peel the shallots, leaving them whole. Peel the garlic and slice finely. Crush the juniper berries, using a pestle and mortar.

4. Melt the butter in a saucepan, add the sliced ordinary onions, garlic and juniper berries and fry gently until golden. Add 300 ml (½ pint) of the vegetable stock and bring to the boil. Season with salt and pepper.

5. Stand the quarter-cut onions upright in a 1.2 litre (2 pint) casserole and add the shallots and sliced spring onions. Spoon the sautéed onion and garlic mixture on top. Cook, uncovered, in the oven for 1½ hours. After halfway through cooking check from time to time that the liquid hasn't dried out and top up with more stock as necessary. At the end of the cooking time the liquid should be thick and syrupy.

6. About 15 minutes from the end of the cooking time, butter the slices of French bread and arrange butter-side up on top of the onion mixture. Sprinkle with the grated cheese and return to the oven to crisp and brown. (If by the end of the cooking time the cheese has not browned, flash the dish under a hot grill for 1-2 minutes.) Sprinkle with the snipped chives and serve immediately, directly from the casserole.

NOTE: The temperature isn't crucial for this dish, so if you are cooking a main course at a higher temperature, simply position the casserole lower in the oven. Check that it doesn't dry out and cover with a lid if necessary.

TECHNIQUE

Quarter four of the onions crosswise through the middle, without cutting right through, so they remain intact during cooking.

ROAST SWEET PEPPERS WITH SAGE

Roast peppers flavoured with fresh herbs make a tasty vegetable accompaniment which will enhance a wide variety of main course dishes. You could even serve them cold as a side salad or starter, if preferred.

SERVES 4

2 large red peppers
2 large orange or yellow
    peppers
1 small onion
1 garlic clove
30 ml (2 tbsp) olive oil
about 8 fresh sage leaves
300 ml (½ pint) vegetable
    stock (see note)
25 g (1 oz) pine nuts
coarse sea salt and pepper

PREPARATION TIME
20 minutes
COOKING TIME
20-25 minutes
FREEZING
Not suitable

170 CALS PER SERVING

1. Preheat the grill to hot, or preheat the oven to 190°C (375°F) Mark 5. Grill or roast the whole peppers on a rack, turning frequently, for 15-20 minutes until the skin is blistered and blackened. Cover with a damp cloth and leave to cool slightly.

2. While the peppers are cooking, peel and chop the onion. Peel and finely slice the garlic. Heat the oil in a small saucepan, add the onion and garlic and cook gently until softened. Add the sage leaves and cook over a moderate heat for 2-3 minutes until frazzled. Remove the sage with a slotted spoon and set aside. Add the vegetable stock to the pan and boil rapidly until reduced to a quarter of the original volume.

3. Spread the pine nuts on a baking sheet and toast in the oven or under the grill for 3-5 minutes, turning frequently, until evenly browned.

4. When the peppers are ready, peel away the skins. Cut off the stalk, then halve the peppers and scrape out the core and seeds. Cut the peppers into broad strips, and add to the garlic and onion mixture. Toss lightly to mix.

5. Arrange the peppers on a warmed serving dish and sprinkle with the pine nuts and sage leaves. Serve immediately.

VEGETABLE STOCK: Use 1 onion, peeled and sliced; 1 leek, cleaned and sliced; 6 spring onion tops, chopped; 1 celery stick, chopped; and 1 carrot, peeled and chopped. Heat 15 ml (1 tbsp) vegetable oil in a saucepan. Add the vegetables and fry gently for 4-5 minutes. Season with salt and pepper, add 1 bay leaf and 1 litre (1¾ pints) water. Bring to the boil and simmer for 20 minutes. Strain, then cool and use as required.

VARIATION

Omit the sage and serve the peppers in a minted cream sauce. Add 200 ml (7 fl oz) crème fraîche and 15 ml (1 tbsp) chopped fresh mint to the reduced stock. Heat through and allow to bubble for about 5 minutes to thicken slightly. Finish as above, garnishing with mint sprigs.

TECHNIQUE

Slice the grilled and skinned peppers into broad strips.

STIR-FRIED SUMMER VEGETABLES

A simple stir-fry is an ideal way to feast on the abundance of summer vegetables. Choose small, tender young vegetables – baby carrots, finger-thick courgettes, slender green beans, mangetouts or sugar snap peas, baby sweetcorn . . . the possibilities are endless! Serve the flavouring sauce separately in a small jug, to allow guests to help themselves.

SERVES 4-6

175 g (6 oz) baby courgettes
  (with flowers if possible)
175 g (6 oz) baby carrots
125 g (4 oz) baby French
  beans
125 g (4 oz) mangetouts or
  sugar snap peas
125 g (4 oz) baby corn cobs
3-4 spring onions
175 g (6 oz) bean sprouts
2.5 cm (1 inch) piece fresh
  root ginger (optional)
1 garlic clove
30 ml (2 tbsp) sunflower oil
30 ml (2 tbsp) light soy sauce
salt and pepper
5-10 ml (1-2 tsp) sesame oil
SAUCE
45 ml (3 tbsp) sherry
45 ml (3 tbsp) light soy sauce
5 ml (1 tsp) thin honey
TO GARNISH
coriander sprigs

PREPARATION TIME
15 minutes
COOKING TIME
5 minutes
FREEZING
Not suitable

195-130 CALS PER SERVING

1. First prepare the vegetables. Halve the courgettes lengthwise. Scrub the carrots and trim, leaving a tuft of stalk on each one. Top and tail the French beans and peas. Halve the baby corn cobs diagonally. Trim the spring onions and shred finely. Rinse the bean sprouts and drain thoroughly.

2. To prepare the sauce, simply mix the sherry, soy sauce and honey together in a small jug; set aside.

3. Peel and finely chop the ginger and garlic. Heat the oil in a wok or large frying pan and add the ginger and garlic to flavour the oil. When the oil is very hot, add the carrots and French beans and fry, turning constantly, for 2-3 minutes.

4. Add the courgettes, mangetouts or sugar snaps, corn cobs, spring onions and bean sprouts, together with the soy sauce. Stir-fry for 2 minutes. Taste and season with salt and pepper if necessary. Sprinkle with the sesame oil. Serve immediately, garnished with coriander sprigs and accompanied by the sauce.

VARIATIONS

Vary the vegetables according to whatever is readily available. Broccoli florets, fine asparagus spears and finely sliced water chestnuts are suitable choices. To serve the stir-fry as a main course, include rice noodles or egg noodles. Cook according to the packet instructions until almost tender. Drain. Add to the stir-fry and cook, turning constantly, for 1 minute. Serve immediately.

TECHNIQUE

Cut the vegetables into similar-sized pieces to ensure that they will cook evenly.

SUGAR SNAP PEAS IN A MINTED LEMON DRESSING

Sugar snap peas are available all year round and make an excellent accompaniment. Here they are served in a light crème fraîche dressing, flavoured with fresh mint and lemon. Fresh peas are equally good served this way – it's well worth seeking them out during their short season or, better still, grow some yourself . . . the flavour of homegrown peas is incomparable.

SERVES 4

400-450 g (14 oz-1 lb) sugar
  snap peas
SAUCE
60 ml (4 tbsp) crème fraîche
15 ml (1 tbsp) finely
  shredded or chopped
  fresh mint
finely pared or grated rind
  and juice of ½ lemon
90 ml (3 fl oz) yogurt
coarse sea salt and pepper
TO GARNISH
mint sprigs

PREPARATION TIME
10 minutes
COOKING TIME
5-10 minutes
FREEZING
Not suitable

105 CALS PER SERVING

1. Top and tail the sugar snap peas, then steam or cook them in boiling water until just tender (see note).

2. Meanwhile gently heat the crème fraîche in a small saucepan, then add the finely chopped mint, lemon rind and juice, stirring gently. When the sauce is warmed through, add the yogurt; do not overheat at this stage otherwise the sauce may curdle. Season with salt and pepper to taste.

3. Drain the sugar snap peas and transfer to a warmed serving dish. Pour over the minted lemon sauce. Garnish with mint sprigs and serve at once.

NOTE: I much prefer to steam sugar snap peas for the shortest possible time to retain their flavour and bite.

VARIATIONS

Instead of sugar snap peas, use mangetouts or fresh peas. You will need 675 g (1½ lb) fresh peas in pods to give the correct shelled weight. Steam or cook in boiling water for 5-10 minutes until tender; continue as above.

  Young broad beans are also delicious steamed and served with this sauce.

TECHNIQUE

Add the mint, lemon rind and juice to the sauce, stirring over a low heat.

SWEDE AND CARROTS WITH MUSTARD SEEDS AND GINGER

Swede has often been a much maligned vegetable, yet it has a distinctive flavour which is enhanced by herbs, spices and aromatic ingredients. Swede and carrots go well together, and the addition of mustard seeds and ginger gives the combination a more exciting aspect!

SERVES 4

450 g (1 lb) swede

450 g (1 lb) carrots

2 pieces preserved stem ginger in syrup, drained

25 g (1 oz) butter

5 ml (1 tsp) black mustard seeds

coarse sea salt and pepper

TO GARNISH

parsley or chervil sprigs

PREPARATION TIME
20 minutes
COOKING TIME
15 minutes
FREEZING
Not suitable

105 CALS PER SERVING

1. Peel the swede and cut into small dice. Peel the carrots and slice thinly. Cook the vegetables separately in boiling salted water until tender.

2. Meanwhile, finely chop the stem ginger. Melt the butter in a small heavy-based saucepan. Add the mustard seeds and heat gently until the seeds begin to pop. Add the chopped ginger and cook for 1 minute over a low heat.

3. Drain the cooked swede and carrots thoroughly, then mash together. Season liberally with freshly ground black pepper and stir in half of the mustard and ginger mixture.

4. Transfer the mashed swede and carrots to a warmed serving dish and drizzle the remaining mustard and ginger mixture over the top. Garnish with parsley or chervil and serve at once.

NOTE: Use a heavy-duty potato masher or a vegetable mill for mashing. Do not use a food processor as this results in an unpleasant glutinous texture.

VARIATION

Make a mustard and ginger cauliflower cheese by tossing cooked cauliflower florets in half of the mustard mixture. Transfer to a gratin dish and spoon on the cheese sauce. Top with the remaining mustard mixture and grated cheese, then brown under the grill.

TECHNIQUE

Mash the carrots and swede together thoroughly, making sure you do not leave any firm lumps.

PARSNIPS IN A LIME GLAZE

The sweet nature of parsnips will complement almost any meal. Here the tang of lime is used to enhance their flavour. If possible, use young tender parsnips. The sharp glaze can be used with any sweet root vegetable to excellent effect – try it with sweet potatoes or carrots, for example.

SERVES 4

675 g (1½ lb) parsnips
1 lime
50 g (2 oz) butter
25 g (1 oz) light muscovado
**   sugar**
coarse sea salt and pepper
TO GARNISH
thyme sprigs

PREPARATION TIME
5 minutes
COOKING TIME
15 minutes
FREEZING
Not suitable

225 CALS PER SERVING

1. Peel the parsnips and trim off the tops and roots. Cut in half lengthways. (If using older, tougher parsnips cut into quarters and remove the woody core.) Add to a pan of boiling salted water and cook for 5 minutes.

2. Meanwhile, using a canelle knife or a vegetable peeler, carefully pare thin slivers of rind from the lime; set aside for the garnish. Halve the lime and squeeze out the juice.

3. Melt the butter in a large saucepan together with the sugar. Add the lime juice and heat gently, stirring, to dissolve the sugar.

4. Drain the parsnips thoroughly in a colander, then add to the lime mixture in the saucepan. Toss in the buttery lime mixture and cook over a moderate heat, shaking the pan frequently, for approximately 10 minutes until golden brown.

5. Transfer to a warmed serving dish and garnish with the slivers of lime zest and thyme sprigs.

VARIATIONS

Replace 1 parsnip with 3 eddoes. Peel and halve the eddoes and cook with the parsnips. Alternatively use carrots or turnips instead of parsnips. A handful of walnuts tossed in towards the end of the cooking time adds a delicious crunch.

TECHNIQUE

Toss the par-boiled parsnips in the buttery lime mixture.

RASPBERRY AND ROSE PETAL TART

Fragrant rose petals transform this raspberry tart into something really special. It is important to choose a highly scented rose which will impart fragrance and flavour. If you would rather have your rose on the sideboard, use rose water instead. Serve the tart warm or cold, with cream or fromage frais.

SERVES 6

PASTRY
125 g (4 oz) plain flour
25 g (1 oz) icing sugar
50 g (2 oz) butter or
 vegetable margarine
1 egg yolk
10-15 ml (2-3 tsp) freshly
 squeezed orange juice
RASPBERRY FILLING
1 medium rose, or 15-30 ml
 (1-2 tbsp) rose water
350 g (12 oz) fresh or frozen
 raspberries
50 g (2 oz) caster sugar
15 ml (1 tbsp) eau de
 framboise or kirsch
CRUMBLE TOPPING
125 g (4 oz) plain flour
25 g (1 oz) cornflour
50 g (2 oz) butter or
 vegetable margarine
25 g (1 oz) granulated sugar
TO FINISH
icing sugar, for dusting
few raspberries, to decorate

PREPARATION TIME
30 minutes
COOKING TIME
35-40 minutes
FREEZING Suitable

470 CALS PER SERVING

1. If using a fresh rose, rinse it briefly under cold running water, taking care to avoid bruising it. Carefully remove the petals. Place the raspberries in a bowl with the sugar, liqueur and rose petals or rose water. Leave to infuse.

2. To make the pastry, sift the flour and icing sugar into a bowl. Cut the butter into pieces and rub into the flour using your fingertips, until the mixture resembles fine breadcrumbs. Using a round-bladed knife, stir in the egg yolk and enough orange juice to bind the pastry to a soft dough. Wrap in cling film and chill in the refrigerator for 20 minutes.

3. Preheat the oven to 200°C (400°F) Mark 6.

4. To make the crumble topping, sift the flour and cornflour into a bowl. Cut the butter into pieces and rub into the flour, using your fingertips, until the mixture resembles coarse breadcrumbs. Stir in the sugar. Cover and chill in the refrigerator.

5. Roll out the pastry on a lightly floured surface and use to line a 20 cm (8 inch) flan tin. Line the pastry case with grease-proof paper and fill with baking beans. Bake the pastry case blind for 10-15 minutes until very faintly coloured. Remove the paper and beans and return to the oven for 5 minutes to lightly cook the base. Lower the oven temperature to 180°C (350°F) Mark 4.

6. Remove the rose petals from the raspberries and set aside for decoration if desired (see note). Fill the pastry case with the raspberries. Top with the crumble mixture, leaving the fruit peeping through in places. Bake in the oven for approximately 30 minutes until the crumble topping is golden brown. Serve warm or cold, dusted with icing sugar and decorated with a few raspberries.

NOTE: Toast the rose petals in the oven while the tart is cooking, until crisp and browned. Arrange on the flan and sprinkle with a little crushed lump sugar.

TECHNIQUE

For the crumble topping, rub the butter into the flour until the mixture resembles coarse breadcrumbs.

CRÊPES WITH ORANGE ICE

This version of the classic French dessert similarly has a spectacular flambéed finish. It is ideal for a dinner party because most of the preparation can be done well ahead; at the last minute, you only need to assemble the dish, heat it through and flambé!

SERVES 6

CRÊPES
125 g (4 oz) plain flour
pinch of salt
2 eggs, beaten
300 ml (½ pint) milk
25 g (1 oz) butter, melted
15 ml (1 tbsp) Grand Marnier
ORANGE ICE CREAM
50 g (2 oz) sugar
finely pared rind and juice of
 1 orange
225 g (8 oz) mascarpone
 cheese
200 g (7 oz) fromage frais
30 ml (2 tbsp) Grand Marnier
SAUCE
25 g (1 oz) unsalted butter
50 g (2 oz) caster sugar
juice of 2 oranges
juice of ½ lemon
30-45 ml (2-3 tbsp) Grand
 Marnier, warmed

PREPARATION TIME
30 minutes
COOKING TIME
About 20 minutes
FREEZING
Suitable: Except sauce

505 CALS PER SERVING

1. First make the ice cream. Put the sugar in a saucepan with 150 ml (¼ pint) water and heat gently until the sugar is dissolved. Add the pared orange rind and boil rapidly until reduced by about half. Remove the orange rind with a slotted spoon, cut into strips and set aside. Add the orange juice to the syrup. Allow to cool.

2. Mix the mascarpone and fromage frais together in a bowl, using a fork. Gradually work in the cooled orange syrup and liqueur. Freeze in an ice cream machine if you have one, according to the manufacturer's directions. Alternatively, turn into a freezerproof container, cover and freeze until firm, whisking occasionally during freezing. Transfer to the refrigerator 30 minutes before serving to soften.

3. To make the crêpe batter, place all the ingredients in a blender or food processor and work until smooth. Alternatively sift the flour and salt into a bowl. Make a well in the centre and add the eggs and half the milk; gradually whisk into the flour. Whisk in the remaining milk, then stir in the butter and liqueur; the batter should have the consistency of single cream.

4. Heat a crêpe pan until very hot and wipe with a little oil. When a light haze forms, pour in just enough batter to thinly coat the base of the pan, tilting the pan to get an even coating. Cook over a fairly high heat until the upper surface looks set and the edges begin to curl. Turn the crêpe over and cook the other side. Transfer to a warmed plate and repeat to make 12 pancakes, interleaving the cooked ones with greaseproof paper.

5. To make the sauce, melt the butter in a large frying pan, add the sugar and heat gently until dissolved, then cook to a golden brown caramel. Carefully add the strained orange and lemon juices and stir until the caramel has dissolved.

6. To serve, place a spoonful or two of ice cream on each crêpe and fold to enclose the filling. Arrange the crêpes in the large frying pan and spoon the sauce over to warm them through. Sprinkle with the orange rind strips. Pour on the liqueur and set alight, shaking the pan gently. Serve immediately.

TECHNIQUE

Lift the crêpe with a palette knife to check whether the underside is cooked, before turning.

MINTED SHORTBREADS WITH SUMMER FRUITS

Shortbread rounds – delicately flavoured with chopped fresh mint – are layered with red, white and black-currants and crème fraîche or thick Greek yogurt, then topped with a liberal dusting of icing sugar. Make this dessert during the short summer currant season, or use frozen summer fruits during the rest of the year. If white currants are unavailable, use the larger quantity of redcurrants.

SERVES 4-6

SHORTBREAD
175 g (6 oz) butter
75 g (3 oz) caster sugar
200 g (7 oz) plain flour
25 g (1 oz) cornflour
15 ml (1 tbsp) finely chopped fresh mint
SUMMER FRUIT FILLING
225-350 g (8-12 oz) redcurrants
225 g (8 oz) blackcurrants
125 g (4 oz) white currants (optional)
15 ml (1 tbsp) caster sugar, or to taste
juice of 1 orange
juice of ½ lemon
15 ml (1 tbsp) white rum or kirsch
TO DECORATE
mint sprigs
icing sugar, for dusting

PREPARATION TIME
30 minutes
COOKING TIME
15-20 minutes
FREEZING
Suitable: Shortbread only

625-430 CALS PER SERVING

1. Preheat the oven to 160°C (325°F) Mark 3.

2. To make the shortbread, cream the butter and sugar together in a bowl until pale and fluffy. Sift in the flour and corn-flour and mix together, using a wooden spoon. Stir in the chopped mint. Use your hands to bring the dough together.

3. Roll out the shortbread dough thinly and cut out eight to twelve 7.5 cm (3 inch) rounds, using a fluted pastry cutter. Carefully transfer to a baking sheet lined with non-stick baking parchment and chill in the refrigerator for 20 minutes. Bake in the oven for 15-20 minutes, until firm and pale golden. Leave on the paper for 5 minutes, then transfer to a wire rack to cool completely.

4. Meanwhile, wash all the currants and remove them from their stalks with a fork, reserving some on stalks for decoration. Place the currants in a pan together with the sugar, orange and lemon juice. Heat gently for a few minutes to slightly soften the fruit. Transfer to a bowl, stir in the rum or kirsch and leave to cool.

5. Assemble the dessert just before serving. Place one shortbread round on each serving plate and cover with the yogurt or crème fraîche and fruit. Top with the remaining shortbread rounds and decorate with sprigs of currants and mint. Dust liberally with icing sugar and serve at once.

NOTE: You may prefer to sweeten the fruit with more sugar than suggested. Personally, I prefer the tart flavour.

VARIATION

Divide the shortbread in half and roll out to two 15 ml (6 inch) rounds. Mark each into eight sections, prick with a fork and bake as above for about 40 minutes; cool. Serve the fruit in a glass bowl, accompanied by the shortbread triangles and yogurt or crème fraîche.

TECHNIQUE

Use a fork to remove the currants from their stalks.

PINEAPPLE AND FIG TART WITH COCONUT PASTRY

This is a fruit tart with the taste of the tropics to conjure up thoughts of warm seas, blue skies and deserted white sandy beaches! A fresh pineapple and fig filling in coconut pastry is hidden by a delicious almond topping. Serve warm, with pouring cream or Greek-style yogurt.

SERVES 6

PASTRY
50 g (2 oz) creamed coconut
175 g (6 oz) plain flour
pinch of salt
100 g (3½ oz) butter or
vegetable margarine
25 g (1 oz) icing sugar
a little freshly squeezed lime
juice, to bind
FILLING
1 small pineapple
3 figs
TOPPING
125 g (4 oz) butter or
vegetable margarine
125 g (4 oz) caster sugar
2 eggs
125 g (4 oz) ground almonds
TO FINISH
icing sugar, for dusting

PREPARATION TIME
30 minutes, plus chilling
COOKING TIME
50-55 minutes
FREEZING
Suitable

730 CALS PER SERVING

1. To make the pastry, dissolve the creamed coconut in 30 ml (2 tbsp) boiling water in a small bowl. Mix to a smooth paste and allow to cool.

2. Sift the flour and salt into a bowl. Cut the butter into pieces and rub into the flour, using your fingertips. Stir in the icing sugar. Using a round-bladed knife, mix in the creamed coconut paste together with the lime juice to form a soft dough. Knead gently in the bowl until smooth. Wrap in cling film and chill in the refrigerator for about 20 minutes.

3. Preheat the oven to 200°C (400°F) Mark 6. Lightly butter a 3 cm (1¼ inch) deep, 23 cm (9 inch) fluted flan tin.

4. Roll out the pastry on a lightly floured surface and use to line the prepared flan tin. Chill again for 20 minutes. Line the pastry case with greaseproof paper or foil and baking beans and bake 'blind' for 10-15 minutes. Remove the paper and beans and return to the oven for 5 minutes to cook the base. Reduce the oven temperature to 180°C (350°F) Mark 4.

5. Meanwhile, cut off the top and bottom of the pineapple and stand it on a board. Cut away the skin, then remove the brown 'eyes' with the tip of a small knife. Quarter the pineapple and cut away the woody core. Cut the flesh into 2 cm (¾ inch) pieces. Halve the figs and scrape out the flesh into a bowl.

6. To make the topping, cream the butter or margarine and sugar together in a bowl using an electric beater or wooden spoon. Beat in the eggs, then stir in the ground almonds. Spread the fig flesh over the base of the pastry case and arrange the pineapple pieces on top. Spread the almond mixture evenly over the filling. Bake in the centre of the oven for 35-40 minutes or until the topping is set. Check after 30 minutes and, if necessary, cover with foil to prevent over-browning.

7. Serve warm, dusted liberally with icing sugar and accompanied by pouring cream or Greek-style yogurt.

TECHNIQUE

Stand the pineapple on a board, then cut away the skin in vertical strips.

SNOW EGGS

Soft, fluffy poached meringues are served on a pool of cool, smooth coffee custard and drizzled with whisky-flavoured chocolate. This simple, yet impressive dessert can be prepared a few hours ahead if preferred; only the chocolate should be applied just before serving.

SERVES 6

10 ml (2 tsp) coffee beans
3 eggs, separated
75 g (3 oz) caster sugar
450 ml (¾ pint) milk
50 g (2 oz) plain chocolate
30 ml (2 tbsp) whisky
blackberries, to decorate
   (optional)

PREPARATION TIME
25 minutes, plus chilling
COOKING TIME
30 minutes
FREEZING
Not suitable

200 CALS PER SERVING

1. Preheat the grill. Spread the coffee beans on a baking sheet and toast for a few minutes, turning frequently.

2. To make the meringue, whisk the egg whites in a large bowl, using an electric beater if possible, until they form firm peaks. Gradually whisk in half of the sugar, a little at a time. Continue whisking until the mixture is stiff and shiny.

3. Pour the milk into a large deep frying pan. Bring to the boil, then reduce the heat to a gentle simmer. Drop five or six spoonfuls of the meringue mixture into the milk, spacing them well apart. Poach gently for about 5 minutes, turning once, until they are firm to the touch. Remove the meringues with a slotted spoon and drain on absorbent kitchen paper. Repeat until all the mixture is used: there should be about 18 meringues in total.

4. Pour the poaching liquid into a saucepan. Whisk the egg yolks and remaining sugar together in a bowl, then whisk in the poaching milk. Return to the pan and add the coffee beans. Stir over a very gentle heat for 10-12 minutes or until slightly thickened to the consistency of double cream, making sure it does not boil.

5. Strain the coffee custard into a serving dish and arrange the meringues on top. Chill in the refrigerator for 15-20 minutes before serving.

6. Melt the chocolate with 15 ml (1 tbsp) water in a heatproof bowl over a pan of hot water. Add the whisky and stir until smooth. Drizzle the whisky-flavoured chocolate over the meringues and decorate with blackberries to serve if wished.

TECHNIQUE

Shape the meringue into ovals, using two tablespoons, then add to the simmering milk.

PETITS POTS DE CREME AU CHOCOLAT

These deliciously rich, smooth chocolate creams are set in special little china pots. If you do not have the traditional custard pots, use small ramekin dishes instead. Serve the *petits pots* with crisp dessert biscuits.

SERVES 6-8

600 ml (1 pint) single cream
2.5 ml (½ tsp) vanilla
   essence
225 g (8 oz) plain chocolate,
   in pieces
1 egg
5 egg yolks
25 g (1 oz) caster sugar
TO DECORATE
whipped cream
cocoa powder, for dusting

PREPARATION TIME
15 minutes, plus chilling
COOKING TIME
About 1 hour
FREEZING
Not suitable

475-355 CALS PER SERVING

1. Preheat the oven to 150°C (300°F) Mark 2. Put the cream, vanilla essence and chocolate into a heavy-based saucepan over a low heat and heat gently, stirring, until the chocolate melts and the mixture is smooth.

2. Lightly mix together the whole egg, egg yolks and caster sugar in a bowl, then stir in the chocolate cream until smooth.

3. Strain the mixture into eight 75 ml (3 fl oz) custard pots, or six ramekins. Cover with lids or small rounds of foil.

4. Stand the custard pots or ramekins in a roasting tin and pour in enough hot water to come halfway up the sides of the dishes. Cook in the oven for about 1 hour until lightly set; the centres should still be slightly soft. Do not overcook or the smooth texture will be spoilt.

5. Remove the pots or ramekins from the tin and allow to cool. Chill before serving, topped with a spoonful of cream and a dusting of cocoa powder.

NOTE: These chocolate pots rely heavily on the flavour of the chocolate used, so it is essential to use a good quality chocolate.

VARIATION

For a less rich version, use half single cream and half milk.

TECHNIQUE

Strain the chocolate mixture through a small sieve into custard pots (or ramekins).

If you would like further information about the **Good Housekeeping Cookery Club**, please write to:
Penny Smith, Ebury Press, Random House, 20 Vauxhall Bridge Road, London SW1V 2SA.